Jacob Have I Loved

by
Katherine Paterson

Student Packet

Written by:
Jean Jamieson

Contains masters for:

1	Prereading Activity
1	Writing Activity
1	Study Guide (4 pages)
1	Literary Analysis Activity
11	Vocabulary Activities
2	Math Activities
1	Descriptive Words Activity
1	Encoded Puzzle Activity
2	Story Review Activities
2	Comprehension Quizzes
1	Novel Test (6 sections, 2 levels)
PLUS	Detailed Answer Key

Note

The text used to prepare this guide was the Harper Trophy softcover edition, © 1980 by Katherine Paterson. The page references may differ in the hardcover or other paperback editions.

ISBN 1-56137-836-4

To order, contact your local
school supply store, or—

Novel Units, Inc.
P.O. Box 791610
San Antonio, TX 78279

What Do You Know About The Chesapeake Bay?

Directions: After reading each of the following statements, write "True" or "False" in the space provided. Make each "false" statement "true" by changing a word, phrase, or the entire statement. If necessary, do some research to determine the correct answer.

1. The Chesapeake Bay is in the United States. _____

2. The Chesapeake Bay is an inlet of the Pacific Ocean. _____

3. The Chesapeake Bay is in Maryland and Virginia. _____

4. The Chesapeake Bay gives deepwater vessels access to important ports. _____

5. The Mississippi River is one of the largest tributary rivers of the Chesapeake Bay. _____

6. There is no bridge or tunnel crossing the Chesapeake Bay._____

7. Ports on the Chesapeake Bay include Newport News and Norfolk in Virginia and Baltimore, Maryland. _____

8. The Chesapeake Bay is an important source of oysters, crabs, and other seafood. _____

9. The Virginia colonist John Adams explored the Chesapeake Bay in 1608. _____

10. The fish and waterfowl of the Chesapeake Bay have been threatened by pollution. _____

Freewriting

Directions: Choose two or more of the following sentence-starts and freewrite for approximately ten minutes. (To freewrite, write without stopping to correct or change anything. Just put your thoughts on the paper.) These thoughts are your own and do not have to be shared. They may be put onto this or a separate sheet of paper, or into a journal.

1. If I had a twin brother or sister _____

_____

_____

_____

2. If I got caught in a hurricane or a tornado_____

_____

_____

_____

3. If everything I owned was damaged so badly it had to be thrown out _____

_____

_____

_____

4. If I had a brother or sister with a special talent_____

_____

_____

_____

5. If an adult that I knew very well made me angry_____

_____

_____

_____

_____

Name_____

Study Questions

Directions: Write a brief answer to each study question as you read the book. Use the questions for review before group discussions and before your final test.

Chapters "Rass Island" & 1–5, pages 1-72

1. In what body of water is Rass Island located? *(page 1)*
2. How does one get from the mainland to Rass Island? *(page 1)*
3. What is the late spring crop of the watermen of Rass Island? *(page 2)*
4. What is the most important thing about the docks of Rass Island? *(page 2)*
5. What type of land makes up most of Rass Island? *(page 3)*
6. As the story begins in Chapter 1, what is the season and the year? *(page 5)*
7. Who is McCall Purnell? *(page 5)*
8. Why does Louise consider Call a good partner on the water? *(pages 7-8)*
9. What does Louise consider to be a defect in Call's character that she must try to correct? *(page 8)*
10. What nickname does Caroline have for Louise? *(page 14)*
11. What does Caroline decide to do with her time during the summer, and why does she make this decision? *(pages 15-16)*
12. What changes the life of Mr. Bradshaw in 1918? *(page 17)*
13. On Rass Island, what represents wealth and security? *(page 18)*
14. What is unique about Caroline's health at her birth? What does she require? *(pages 18-20)*
15. Although she wants to join her father who works on the water, why is Louise not allowed to do it? *(page 21)*
16. What is Louise's consolation for not being allowed to go aboard the *Portia Sue* as her father's deckhand? *(page 21)*
17. How does Susan Bradshaw manage to barter for piano lessons for the twins? What else is included in the barter? *(pages 22-23)*
18. What is Caroline's "true gift"? *(page 23)*
19. How does Mr. Rice help Caroline obtain voice lessons? *(page 24)*
20. What announcement does Louise hear broadcast on the radio on Sunday, December 7, 1941? *(page 27)*
21. What simple thing does Susan Bradshaw do on the night of December 7, 1941 that makes the twins realize that their secure world is "forever in the past"? *(page 29)*

---

22. What does Louise propose be done about the Christmas concert of 1941? How is the proposal received? *(pages 30-31)*
23. How much baggage does the stranger on the ferry bring to the island? What does it indicate to the people of Rass Island? *(page 49)*
24. Who is the stranger from the ferry? *(page 54)*
25. How are Louise and Call greeted by the stranger as they investigate his house? *(pages 66-67)*
26. How does the stranger make Call laugh? *(page 69)*
27. What name do Louise and Call decide to use for the stranger? *(page 71)*

Chapters 6–10, pages 73-125
28. Why does Louise hate Caroline? *(page 74)*
29. What plan does Louise formulate to escape the island? *(pages 76-77)*
30. What contest does Louise enter? *(page 78)*
31. What do Call and Louise decide to do for the Captain? *(pages 88-89)*
32. What is Louise's least favorite winter month? Why? *(page 91)*
33. What is Louise's least favorite summer month? Why? *(page 92)*
34. What is the Captain's one concession to working in the August heat? *(page 93)*
35. What kind of letter does Louise receive from the contest sponsor? *(pages 93-94)*
36. What does the Captain do that makes Louise laugh? *(page 96)*
37. What does the Captain call Auntie Braxton? How does this make Louise feel? *(page 97)*
38. What does Louise discover when she tries to return the cat to Auntie Braxton? *(page 98)*
39. Is Auntie Braxton dead? *(page 99)*
40. How does the Captain confirm himself to be the true Hiram Wallace to the people on the island? *(pages 100-101)*
41. What is the biggest problem facing the Captain, Call and Louise when it comes to cleaning the Braxton house? *(page 102)*
42. What is the initial decision made regarding Auntie's cats? *(page 105)*
43. What is Caroline's suggestion as to the disposal of the cats? Does it work? *(pages 112-114)*
44. What are some things the Bradshaws do to prepare for the anticipated hurricane? *(pages 115-117)*
45. Where does the Captain sit out the storm? *(page 120)*
46. What does Caroline do during the hurricane? *(page 122)*
47. What happens to the island cat population because of the storm? *(page 125)*

Chapters 11–15, pages 126-193

48. Why do you think Louise loves everyone on the morning after the hurricane? *(page 130)*
49. What is the condition of the Captain's property after the storm? *(page 130)*
50. What is the most vital thing the Bradshaws need to know after the storm? *(page 135)* Why do you think that is so?
51. How long does the Captain live with the Bradshaws after the storm? *(page 139)*
52. What arrangements does the Captain make with Trudy Braxton? *(pages 144-145)*
53. What is Louise's theory about the most revealing part of the human body? Do you agree or disagree? Why? *(page 147)*
54. Why do you think Louise gets so upset when Caroline uses her lotion without asking? *(pages 148-149)*
55. What is your opinion of Louise's behavior? Do you think she is "going crazy"? *(page 150)*
56. What is Louise's assessment of the treatment accorded harmless "crazy people"? *(page 151)* Do you agree or disagree with her? Why?
57. What proposal does Caroline make to the Captain concerning his lack of housing? *(page 157)* What is Caroline's strongest "selling point"? *(page 158)*
58. What effect does the Captain's marriage have on Louise? *(page 162)*
59. What does Caroline do when she and Call visit the Captain and Trudy almost every day? *(page 167)*
60. Why does Call drop out of school in February? What does he do? *(page 171)*
61. What changes does this work bring about in Call? *(page 172)*
62. What does the Captain propose to do with Trudy's legacy? *(pages 176-177)*
63. What effect does the Captain's proposal have on Louise? *(page 180)*
64. What does Susan Bradshaw offer to Louise? How does Louise respond to the offer? *(page 182)*
65. What responsibility does Louise take over after Call joins the navy? *(page 183)* What does this do to her education? *(page 185)*
66. What gives Louise some happiness during the winter months? *(pages 187-188)*
67. What is the difference in the aftermath of dredging and tonging for oysters? What is your opinion of these methods? *(page 189)*
68. What is done about Louise's education? *(pages 191-192)*

Chapters 16–20, pages 194-244

69. How has Call changed during the time he has been in the Navy? *(page 201)*
70. What is Call's prediction for the future of Rass Island? *(page 202)*
71. What is Call's assessment of what Louise thought of him? *(page 208)* Do you think he is accurate? Why or why not?
72. Why doesn't Louise attend the wedding of Caroline and Call? *(pages 209-210)*
73. What does Louise learn about the past relationship of the Captain and her grandmother? *(pages 211-212 & 215)*
74. What is the Captain's assessment of Louise? *(pages 216-218)* Do you agree or disagree with him? Why?
75. What kind of relationship is inferred between Mr. and Mrs. Bradshaw? *(pages 219-221)*
76. How do you think Louise feels about the choices her mother has made in her lifetime? Why do you think Louise feels as she does? *(pages 224-226)*
77. What does Louise want from her mother? *(pages 226-227)*
78. What initial decision does Louise make about her future? *(pages 229-230)* Why is she forced to change her plans? *(page 231)*
79. Where does Louise decide to locate after graduation, and why? *(pages 231-232)*
80. Why is the school in Truitt larger than the one on Rass Island? *(page 232)* What is your opinion of the basis used for the determinant of "wealth" in the Appalachian wilderness? *(page 232)*
81. What is the most pressing health problem in Truitt? How does Louise compare the mountain men of Truitt to the water men of Rass Island? *(page 233)*
82. How does Louise meet Joseph Wojtkiewicz? *(page 234)*
83. What does Joseph surmise from Louise's background? *(page 236)*
84. What conclusion does Louise make about Joseph at their first meeting? Why? *(page 237)*
85. Why do you think Louise feels that the people of Truitt have not only accepted her in their lives, they have taken her into their hearts? *(page 240)* What do you think is the difference?
86. Why do you think Louise is so adamant about the survival of the second twin? *(page 242)*
87. What do you think is the meaning of the last paragraph of the novel? *(page 244)*
88. What is your opinion as to why the author gave the title *Jacob Have I Loved* to this novel?

Similes

Directions: At times authors use figurative language to make descriptions more vivid for readers. <u>Similes</u> are comparisons using such words as *like, as, similar to, resembles,* etc. For example: *She is as happy as a lark.*

Below are some similes used by Katherine Paterson in *Jacob Have I Loved.* Analyze each simile by telling what two things are being compared and how they are alike.

1. "The ferry will be almost there before I can see Rass, lying low as a terrapin back on the faded olive water of the Chesapeake." (page 1)

_____ is like_____

because_____

2. "I obeyed, pinning the straps [of the overalls] securely to the clothesline. Immediately, the breeze took them straight out, as though Peter Pan had donned them to fly across our yard toward never-never land across the Bay." (page 14)

_____ is like _____

because_____

3. "...I see the face of old Auntie Braxton, as she stands stock still in front of our picket fence, lips parted to reveal her almost toothless gums, eyes shining, drinking in a polonaise as though it were heavenly nourishment." (page 23)

_____ is like_____

because_____

4. "Tiny little one-syllable explosions went off about the room like a string of Chinese firecrackers. Mr. Rice looked stern." (page 30)

_____ is like_____

because_____

Vocabulary—Synonym or Antonym?

Vocabulary Words			
distinctive 2	delusions 5	precarious 7	avid 10
benevolently 14	strenuously 17	meager 17	exquisite 20
bewildered 20	affluent 23	vulgar 23	rankle 25

Directions: Match the synonym or antonym in the comparison with a listed vocabulary word.

Example: GOOD is to BAD as BETTER is to WORSE.

1. SERENE is to CALM as _____ is to CONFUSED.

2. SLOW is to FAST as _____ is to ADEQUATE.

3. HEADSTRONG is to STUBBORN as _____ is to PROSPEROUS.

4. SCOLD is to CHIDE as _____ is to MISCONCEPTIONS.

5. SCOWL is to SMILE as _____ is to ORDINARY.

6. MISERY is to HAPPINESS as _____ is to PLEASE.

7. HUMILIATED is to EMBARRASSED as _____ is to ENTHUSIASTIC.

8. GENTLY is to HARSHLY as _____ is to REFINED.

9. ORNATE is to PLAIN as _____ is to UNKINDLY.

10. STAY is to REMAIN as _____ is to UNSTABLE.

11. TORMENT is to BOTHER as _____ is to ENERGETICALLY.

12. GALLED is to RANKLED as _____ is to ELEGANT.

Name_____

Scrambled Words

Vocabulary Words			
semblance 2	deceptively 2	emphatic 12	benevolently 14
undaunted 15	consolation 21	lugubriously 22	coincidences 24

Directions: Unscramble each word. Draw a line to the definition. Include each word in a sentence.

Scrambled Words	Unscrambled Words	Definitions
1. d d u u t e a n n	_____	a. appearance
2. t h a i e m c p	_____	b. seemingly
3. m n l e e a b c s	_____	c. accentuated
4. s n n e e c c c i i o d	_____	d. kindly
5. c l y e e e i d t v p	_____	e. resolute
6. g r y o u u u i l l b s	_____	f. assuagement
7. v l l e e e o y b n n t	_____	g. dismally
8. s c i o o o a n n l t	_____	h. chances

Sentences:

_____
_____
_____
_____
_____
_____
_____
_____

Kriss Kross Vocabulary

remote 26	grotesque 28	quibble 28	petulant 29
discomfited 30	indignation 31	reprimand 32	frivolous 33
purged 35	trounced 35	pretentious 37	immune 41
passive 43	emerged 47	exasperated 50	melancholy 51
lavishly 54	feats 60	retort 65	significance 70

Directions: Write the vocabulary word that matches each synonym–antonym clue. Be sure to check the pages given to determine the meaning of the word used by the author. Fit the vocabulary words into the Kriss Kross grid that follows.

	Synonym	Antonym	Vocabulary Word
1.	impractical	practical	_____
2.	ugly	natural	_____
3.	importance	unimportance	_____
4.	came out	left	_____
5.	embarrassed	soothed	_____
6.	profusely	scarcely	_____
7.	removed	close	_____
8.	unaffected	susceptible	_____
9.	bicker	agree	_____
10.	infuriate	calmed	_____
11.	admonishment	commendation	_____
12.	achievements	failures	_____
13.	inactive	dynamic	_____
14.	anger	happiness	_____
15	crabby	pleasant	_____
16.	sadness	happiness	_____
17.	snappy answer	question	_____

Vocabulary Kriss Kross

Directions: Fit the vocabulary words into the following blank puzzle structure.

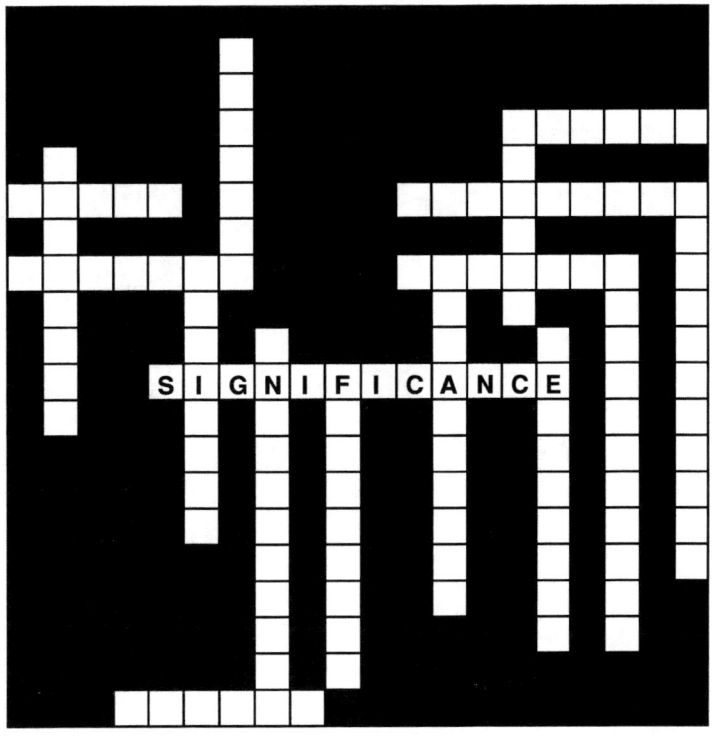

Directions: Use as many of the Kriss Kross words as possible in a short written paragraph.

_____

_____

_____

_____

_____

_____

_____

_____

_____

Blending Syllables

Directions: To do this activity, choose one group of letters from Column A, one from Column B, and one from Column C. Do this fifteen times to form a set of long vocabulary words. The first one is done for you. In each column every letter group should be used only once.

Column A	Column B	Column C	Completed Vocabulary Word
ter	sump	sions	1. **terrapin**
dis	phat	strance	2. _____
de	lo	tive	3. _____
con	qui	ed	4. _____
loo	u	ly	5. _____
em	**ra**	dered	6. _____
lob	ri	tion	7. _____
un	mon	naise	8. _____
ex	tinc	**pin**	9. _____
be	ni	ate	10. _____
po	daunt	ic	11. _____
re	lu	lant	12. _____
pet	di	ness	13. _____
me	wil	mand	14. _____
rep	lol	site	15. _____

Expanding Words

Directions: Each of the words between the blank lines can be expanded into a vocabulary word by adding letters before and after the word. Use one letter per blank.

Short Word	**Expanded Vocabulary Word**
__ RIM __ __	1. __ __ __ __ __ __
__ __ __ TIN __ __ __ __ __	2. __ __ __ __ __ __ __ __ __ __ __
__ RACK __ __ __	3. __ __ __ __ __ __ __ __
__ __ __ AN __ __	4. __ __ __ __ __ __ __
__ __ __ SUM __ __ __ __	5. __ __ __ __ __ __ __ __ __ __
__ __ __ CAR __ __ __	6. __ __ __ __ __ __ __ __ __
__ __ __ NINE __ __	7. __ __ __ __ __ __ __ __
__ __ WAR __	8. __ __ __ __ __
__ __ __ AUNT __ __	9. __ __ __ __ __ __ __ __
__ ASK __ __ __	10. __ __ __ __ __ __ __
__ __ __ SEAT __ __	11. __ __ __ __ __ __ __ __
__ __ RAP __ __ __	12. __ __ __ __ __ __
__ __ AGE __	13. __ __ __ __ __
__ __ WILD __ __	14. __ __ __ __ __ __ __
__ __ FLUE __ __	15. __ __ __ __ __ __ __

Vocabulary

terrapin 1	primly 2	spindly 2	semblance 2
distinctive 2	deceptively 2	brackish 3	delusions 5
consumption 7	psychiatrist 9	thwart 13	basking 15

Directions: Find the missing word for each clue. Write the letters of a vocabulary word that is a synonym for the word that is given in the spaces provided. Then transfer the numbered letters to the numbered spaces at the end of the activity. Complete the quote.

1. hinder

   __ __ __ __ __
   4 5 15 13   12

2. misconceptions

   __ __ __ __ __ __ __ __
   19   3   2 18

3. delighting

   __ __ __ __ __ __
   8 7

4. properly

   __ __ __ __ __ __
   11 6 9 14 1

5. depletion

   __ __ __ __ __ __ __ __ __
   10   17   16

Complete the quote. On page 215, Captain Wallace tells Louise, "It's so good to be old,

                                    "

__ __ __ __ __ __ __ __ __ __ __ __ __ __ __ __ __ __ __
1 2 3 4 5   6 7   8   9 10 11 12 13 14 15 16 17 18 19

What do you think Captain Wallace means by that statement?

_____

_____

_____

_____

_____

Puzzlement—Which Vocabulary Word Is it?

coincidences 24	machinations 26	remonstrance 28	indignation 31
pretentious 37	precariously 49	undefinable 58	incredible 60
significance 70	formulated 76	contemplate 77	squandered 78
boomerang 80	ramshackle 86	scavengers 92	fascinated 95
unproscribed 96	interloper 97	irreverent 97	dilapidated 98

Directions: The object of this activity is to discover the vocabulary word from whose letters other words are made. Read the clue words given. Decide which of the vocabulary words listed above furnish the letters for the clue words. The first one is done for you.

Clue Words	Number Of Letters In Word	Word
1. rope, lint, rent, nip, pet	10	interloper
2. tint, post, rest, nose, sue	11	_____
3. mate, rule, form, deaf, left	10	_____
4. tape, dial, lap, date, dip	11	_____
5. chin, son, match, ham, notch	12	_____
6. face, nice, sign, can, gas	12	_____
7. scrub, nose, rip, bud, crib	12	_____
8. monster, race, near, stem, tear	12	_____
9. find, bun, fable, deaf, nine	11	_____
10. cake, lash, mark, harm, shame	10	_____

Directions: Create three Puzzlements from the remaining vocabulary words. Trade with a partner.

Name_____

Vocabulary Crossword

Directions: Read the clues to figure out where to put the vocabulary words on the puzzle.

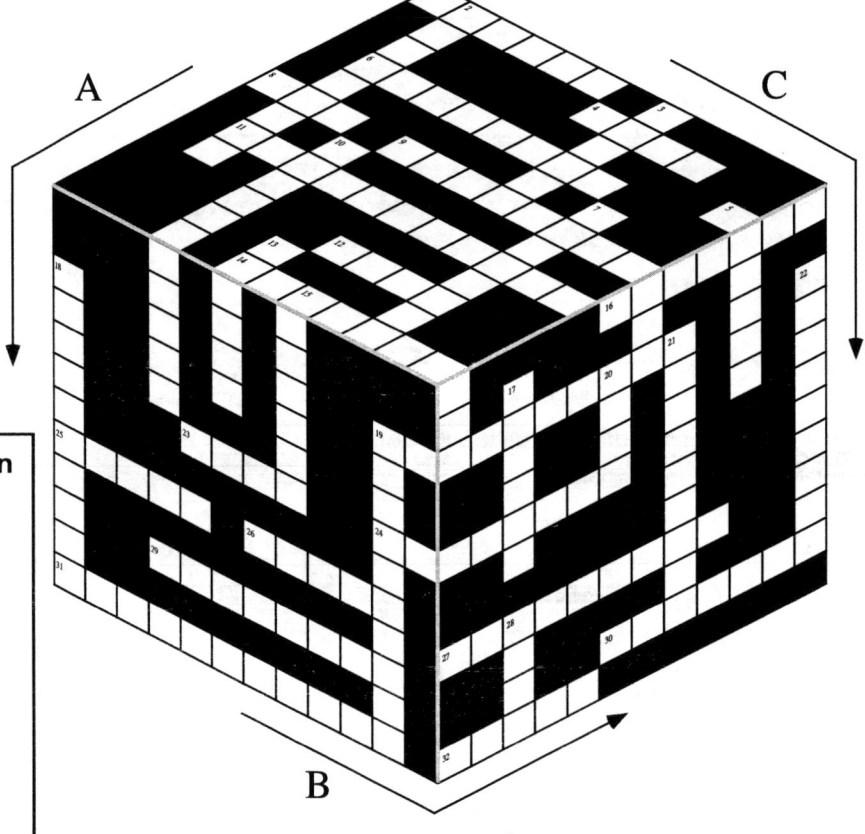

Clues in the "C" direction
1) answerable
4) oppose
5) strong
6) attempt
8) sarcastic
9) think about seriously
11) dangerous
12) very tiny bit
14) meddler
17) cleaned, purified
20) rigid, tight
21) imperfect
22) hateful
28) achievement

Clues in the "A" direction
2) honor
3) snappy answer
7) pretender
10) spruced up
13) invocation
15) disaster
18) frittered away
19) captivated

Clues in the "B" direction
16) rough sounding
19) concocted
23) clever
24) scorn
25) first public appearance
26) devilish being or influence
27) confused
29) prosperous
30) pathetic
31) falling apart
32) essential

Synonym Chains

passive 43	robust 47	exasperated 50	melancholy 51
lavishly 54	cunning 61	flounced 68	fickle 77
ramshackle 86	deficient 89	malicious 91	irreverent 97
dilapidated 98	hysterical 105	wily 107	piteous 108
ominous 115	treacherous 120	taut 128	raucous 129

Directions: Make a chain of synonyms leading from one word to a different word that is not a synonym of the first word. Choose a vocabulary word from those listed above. Write a synonym for that word. Continue giving a synonym for the synonym until you no longer have a synonym for the vocabulary word. Make at least <u>six</u> synonym chains. Use a dictionary or thesaurus if necessary.

For example: <u>flounced</u> - bounced - ejected - banished

1. _____

2. _____

3. _____

4. _____

5. _____

6. _____

7. _____

19

Missing Vowels (A-E-I-O-U)

Directions: Fill in the missing vowels (A-E-I-O-U) of the following vocabulary words. The consonants shown are in their proper order. The first one is done for you.

Consonants	Vocabulary Word	Consonants	Vocabulary Word
SVGRY	1. SAVAGERY	FLS	10. _____
RSSNG	2. _____	TRGDY	11. _____
PRSSY	3. _____	DSMBDD	12. _____
DND	4. _____	FLTHST	13. _____
DLCCY	5. _____	HWKNG	14. _____
RMPGS	6. _____	DSTTT	15. _____
MLT	7. _____	JPRDY	16. _____
RSD	8. _____	SLSHNG	17. _____
TNDRL	9. _____	MRVLSLY	18. _____

Directions: Define <u>six</u> of the vocabulary words used in this activity.

1. _____

2. _____

3. _____

4. _____

5. _____

6. _____

Extra Money

Directions: Read the following problems and calculate the answers.

The piano tuner comes to the island once a month to tune the Bradshaw's piano and to give piano lessons to Louise, Caroline, and other island children. The island children pay the Bradshaws to practice on their piano. (pages 22-23)

1. The Bradshaws receive twenty cents a week from each child. They receive a total of eighty cents a week. How many children are paying? _____

2. If there are fifty-two weeks in a year, how much money do the Bradshaws receive from the children in a year? _____

3. Each child pays the teacher fifty cents for the lesson. How much money does the piano teacher earn each month from the children? _____

4. How much money does the piano teacher earn in one year from the children?
_____

5. How much money does each child pay for lessons and practice a month if there are four weeks in the month? _____ …if there are five weeks in the month?
_____

6. Louise and Call are paid fifty cents for the one terrapin they caught, which is ten times the price they are paid for a soft shell crab. They split the money equally. (pages 7 and 13) Louise gives her mother the money she receives, $2.45. How much are they paid for each soft shell crab? _____ How many soft shell crabs have Louise and Call caught on that day? _____

7. If Louise had to pay for her piano lessons, how many soft shell crabs would Louise and Call have to catch to pay for one lesson? _____

8. If Caroline went crabbing with Louise and Call, and they shared the crab money equally, how many crabs would the three of them have to catch for Louise to pay for one piano lesson? _____

9. How many crabs would you have to catch for enough money to do or purchase three of your favorite things? List the price of each. List the number of crabs caught if you went crabbing alone. List the number if you went crabbing with two friends.

Follow That Crab!

Directions: Imagine you are following the crabs that Louise and Call caught. Make the calculations as indicated in the steps that follow.

1. Louise and Call sell the crabs to Otis for five cents each, making the value of each crab five cents. (page 13) Imagine that Otis triples the cost of each crab as he sells them to a distributor on the mainland. This makes the value of each crab $\underline{\hspace{1.5cm}}

   The value of one crab has increased by what percent of the original value of 5 cents? _____ %

2. Imagine that the distributor on the mainland sells some of the crabs to a restaurant supplier. Each crab is sold for thirty cents. How much has one crab increased in value from the distributor to the restaurant supplier? _____ %

   What is the percent of increase of one crab between the original value of 5 cents and the restaurant supplier? _____ %

3. Imagine that the restaurant supplier sells the crabs to a seafood restaurant. The restaurant features a New England crab boil, selling each cooked crab for $1.25. What is the increase in the amount of value of each five cent crab? $\underline{\hspace{2cm}}

   What is the percent of increase in value between the restaurant supplier and the seafood restaurant? _____ %

   What is the percent of increase in value between the five cent crab and the $1.25 crab? _____ %

   If the current price of a boiled crab is $2.75, what would be the percent of increase between the $2.75 and $1.25 boiled crab? _____ %

Directions: Imagine that you are an employee of an advertising agency. Your assignment is to create a one-eighth page advertisement for the crab boil for the seafood restaurant to place in the newspaper. Use a separate piece of paper for your advertisement.

Words and Phrases

wily 107	feat 114	floes 127	gut 127
taut 128	vital 135	whit 146	prissy 146
verge 151	moult 184	sook 184	alien 186
spat 189	wry 198	gaudy 213	brink 222
defy 224	iota 227	soothe 235	debut 239

Directions: Devise a phrase consisting of words beginning with the letters of at least <u>six</u> of the vocabulary words listed above. (The phrase does not have to pertain to the story.) For example:

Word Chosen   **Phrase Created**
_____

FLOES   FINALLY LOUISE OVERCOMES EARLY STRUGGLES
_____

_____

_____

_____

_____

_____

_____

_____

_____

_____

Cryptogram

Directions: Decode the following to find out how Louise feels when her college advisor recommends that she change her major from premed to nursing. (page 230)

Instructions For Cryptogram Decoding: To decode the following cryptogram, you will need to discover the code used to encrypt the quote. Use the hints given to determine the code. Then use the code to decipher the quote. Fill in the letter above the line that corresponds to the code representation below the line.

CODE: D = A, X = U, and W = T.

_____ , _____ _ _____ _____ , _____ _ ____

OLIH,   OLNH   D   FUDE   SRW,   FDWFKHV   D   ORW

__ _____ ____ _____ ' _ _____ ____ .

RI   WUDVK   BRX   KDYHQ'W   EDUJDLQHG   IRU.

Directions: Use a different statement from the book, or a thought of your own. Encode it with your own cryptogram code. Give clues to your code, and trade with a partner.

A	B	C	D	E	F	G	H	I	J	K	L	M

N	O	P	Q	R	S	T	U	V	W	X	Y	Z

Vocabulary Word Search

Directions: Do the word search. Find the words that may be printed forwards, backwards, horizontally, and on a diagonal. Write down the letters that have not been used, starting at the top and working left to right in each row. Group the letters into words to find the hidden message. (Let X represent a period.)

H	E	S	A	D	C	S	U	R	N	A	M	E	L	O	O	L	T	K	L	S	E
E	D	L	H	D	R	I	I	K	E	S	I	L	A	V	I	R	G	O	E	M	P
L	E	E	T	R	A	A	N	F	L	O	E	S	H	T	O	N	B	M	B	R	D
I	U	E	X	E	A	M	W	O	D	I	V	A	A	U	I	L	B	A	E	E	O
P	N	G	T	Q	K	P	A	E	R	E	K	N	N	G	O	L	T	C	L	M	P
T	R	T	U	U	U	A	N	N	E	I	Y	C	G	L	A	T	A	F	I	R	R
A	R	I	E	B	T	I	S	E	T	L	E	O	L	N	L	R	F	N	I	I	E
U	O	N	M	R	R	I	S	E	L	D	R	Y	C	E	I	A	O	S	D	O	T
T	B	F	G	L	L	I	T	I	M	P	M	E	D	O	B	U	S	W	D	A	O
Y	U	G	N	N	Y	O	O	S	T	A	W	H	U	B	S	Y	O	H	R	T	R
L	S	N	A	W	O	S	P	U	E	E	N	S	E	U	S	R	L	I	A	E	T
D	T	I	W	D	A	D	S	E	S	D	S	N	S	B	S	U	E	T	H	R	Y
N	I	K	T	U	E	T	N	B	R	L	E	A	N	N	E	U	O	V	S	G	L
I	G	E	C	L	A	O	R	E	B	V	Y	D	B	T	I	D	O	C	A	E	I
P	T	I	O	C	C	A	S	O	O	R	R	A	E	O	N	P	E	E	U	U	W
S	L	J	C	T	C	I	O	L	E	R	I	E	L	L	T	A	A	V	T	A	Q
Y	A	A	U	K	A	M	E	L	E	O	T	V	H	E	D	E	L	R	I	I	R
C	T	R	I	N	E	N	B	V	V	Y	F	E	D	U	P	W	D	U	U	R	L	P
O	N	S	O	R	T	B	E	H	Y	N	O	R	I	L	I	I	U	R	T	E	E
E	H	L	A	L	I	R	D	E	B	U	T	O	Y	S	E	C	V	F	S	E	T
T	O	N	Y	U	I	R	A	N	K	L	E	I	O	T	A	T	E	E	E	E	P
P	G	R	Q	E	S	E	C	N	A	R	T	S	N	O	M	E	R	D	S	B	X

ADAMANT	PITEOUS
ALEWIVES	POLONAISE
AVID	PRECARIOUS
BAFFLED	PRIMLY
BEDEVIL	PRISSY
BEFUDDLED	PROGGING
BENEVOLENTLY	QUAVER
BOOMERANG	QUIBBLE
BRACKISH	RANKLE
CAJOLED	RAUCOUS
DEBUT	REMONSTRANCE
DECIPHER	RETORT
DEFY	REVERIE
DESTITUTE	RIVULET
EGRET	ROBUST
EKING	SABOTEURS
EMBATTLED	SAUCILY
EXQUISITE	SEMBLANCE
FLOES	SHARD
INTERLOPER	SHRAPNEL
IOTA	SPINDLY
IRONIC	STACCATO
IRONY	SURNAME
LEEWARD	TAUT
LITANY	TERRAPIN
LOBLOLLY	TROUNCED
LUGUBRIOUSLY	TWANG
NAMESAKE	VALISE
NOCTURNE	WHIT
OMINOUS	WILY
PETULANT	

Hidden Message: (Louise's impression of Joseph on the day she treated his son, Stephen, for an earache. page 237)

_____

_____

_____

Story Review

Directions: Answer each question by circling the letter in the YES or NO column.

		<u>YES</u>	<u>NO</u>
1.	Louise and Caroline are twins.	O	X
2.	Caroline is the older twin	Z	N
3.	Rass Island is located in the water of Chesapeake Bay.	I	B
4.	Crabs and oysters are the crop of the Rass watermen.	T	Y
5.	The story begins in the year 1991.	V	H
6.	Most of Rass Island is salt water marsh.	U	J
7.	Call is twenty-one when the story begins.	K	D
8.	Louise's true gift is her voice.	L	F
9.	Hiram Wallace moves back to Rass Island.	E	P
10.	Hiram Wallace marries Susan Bradshaw.	X	R
11.	Rass Island is hit by a hurricane.	W	Q
12.	Louise attends a high school in Baltimore.	R	A
13.	Call joins the Navy.	S	C
14.	Call marries Caroline.	G	Z
15.	Louise stays on Rass Island for her entire life.	A	M
16.	Louise marries Jacob.	Y	C

Directions: Louise wants to know why her mother stayed on Rass Island as a teacher when she wanted to go to Paris "to find herself." Fill in the circled letters that correspond to the numbered question to learn what Susan Bradshaw replies to Louise's question: "And did you find yourself here on this little island?" (page 225)

"

__ __ __ __ __ __ __ __ __ __ __ __ __ __ __ __ __ __ __ __ __ __ __ __ __ __ __

3 8 1 6 2 7   4 5 9 10 9   11 12 13   2 1 4 5 3 2 14 15 6 16 5

"

__ __ __ __ __ __ __ .

4 1   8 3 2 7

What do you think Susan Bradshaw means by her reply? _____

_____

_____

Story Review Crossword Puzzle

Directions: Use the clues to figure out the answers to the crossword puzzle.

Across
6 lady with cats (2 words)
9 Susan's former profession
10 Louise's nickname
11 musical instrument in Bradshaw home
13 first name of older twin
15 Mrs. Bradshaw's first name
16 spring/summer crop of the watermen
17 fall/winter crop of the watermen
20 name of music school in New York
21 branch of service Call joins
22 Louise moves to this kind of community
23 name of water in which island is located
   (2 words)

Down
1 Call's age when story begins
2 Louise's profession
3 the identity of the captain (2 words)
4 Mr. Bradshaw's first name
5 first name of Louise's husband
7 name of Bradshaw's boat (2 words)
8 Louise's age when story begins
12 boat going between island and mainland
14 name of island where story takes place
18 Auntie's first name
19 first name of younger twin

Name_____

True–False Comprehension Quiz

Directions: Label each statement "T" for true or "F" for false. Correct all false statements to make them true.

_____ 1. Rass Island is located in the water of the Chesapeake Bay.

_____ 2. Caroline Bradshaw is telling the story.

_____ 3. Call and Caroline are twins.

_____ 4. Louise is thirteen when the story begins.

_____ 5. Louise and Call go crabbing together to earn money.

_____ 6. Louise and Caroline both take trumpet lessons.

_____ 7. The stranger on the ferry turns out to be Truitt Bradshaw.

_____ 8. Louise doesn't like it when Caroline will not fight with her.

_____ 9. Caroline enters a lyric-writing contest.

_____ 10. Call and Louise help the Captain restore his house.

_____ 11. Susan discovers Auntie Braxton on the floor of her home when she goes to return a cat to Auntie.

_____ 12. The Captain calls Auntie Braxton "Trudy."

_____ 13. Call, Caroline and Louise give away Auntie Braxton's cats.

_____ 14. Grandma Bradshaw sleeps through the hurricane of '42.

_____ 15. The Captain sits out the hurricane at the Bradshaw house.

Short Answer Comprehension Quiz

Directions: Answer each question in one complete sentence.

1. What is the condition of the Captain's property after the storm?

2. What housing arrangements does the Captain make with Trudy Braxton after the storm?

3. When Trudy is due to return to the island, what does Caroline encourage the Captain to do?

4. What effect does the Captain's marriage have on Louise?

5. Why does Call drop out of school in February to work for Mr. Bradshaw?

6. What does the Captain propose to do with Trudy's legacy?

7. What responsibility does Louise take over after Call joins the Navy?

8. What is done about Louise's high school education?

9. What is Call's prediction for the future of Rass Island when he sees it upon his return?

10. Why doesn't Louise attend the wedding of Caroline and Call?

11. How does Louise break away from the island?

12. Why is Louise forced to change her plans about becoming a doctor?

13. Where does Louise locate after graduating from college?

14. What is the most pressing heath problem in Louise's new home town?

15. What is Louise's conclusion about Joseph at their first meeting?

Vocabulary

Directions: Draw a dotted line around the pair of words in each group that are *opposite* in meaning. Draw a solid line around the pair of words in each group that are *similar* in meaning.

1. terrapin   distinctive   deceptively
    semblance   unique   honestly

2. avid   thwart   brackish
    enthusiastic   help   progging

3. benevolently   delusions   undaunted
    unkindly   finance   resolute

4. hoarded   meager   precarious
    stockpiled   adequate   looniness

5. psychiatrist   strenuously   bewildered
    loblolly   lethargically   confused

6. affluent   grotesque   basking
    prosperous   beautiful   nauseated

7. quibble   shrapnel   rankle
    agree   eking   annoy

8. petulant   robust   cajoled
    pleasant   strong   tonging

9. polonaise   exasperated   fickle
    coincidences   upset   reliable

10. significance   fervent   malicious
    importance   reprimand   kind

Identification By Clues

Directions: Find a character on the right who matches the description on the left. Write the letter of the character next to the matching number. Each character is to be used only once.

_____	1.	She taught school on the island before marrying a waterman.	a. Louise
			b. Auntie Braxton
_____	2.	He lived with his mother and grandmother on the island before joining the Navy.	c. Susan Bradshaw
			d. Joseph
_____	3.	He returns to the island after many years.	e. Truitt Bradshaw
_____	4.	She sits in her rocking chair and criticizes others.	f. Captain Wallace
			g. Call
_____	5.	She is the twin with the good singing voice.	h. Caroline
_____	6.	She has many cats.	i. Grandma Bradshaw
_____	7.	He is a waterman.	
_____	8.	She becomes a nurse-midwife.	
_____	9.	He lives in the mountains.	

Directions: Choose one of the characters. Write a description of that character. Give your opinion of that character.

_____

_____

_____

_____

_____

Identification By Quotation

Directions: Find a character on the right who matches the quote on the left. Write the letter of the character next to the matching number. Use each character only once.

_____ 1. "I'm not going to rot here like Grandma. I'm going to get off this island and do something." (page 226)

_____ 2. "Can't have no yelling. You can't have a body yelling at you when you're trying to eat." (page 213)

_____ 3. "I chose the island. I chose to leave my own people and to build a life for myself somewhere else." (page 227)

_____ 4. "Well, if it isn't Wheeze and Cough." (page 86)

_____ 5. "The boat's all right...There's plenty that aren't so lucky." (page 135)

_____ 6. "No, Grandma, remember, I told you Betty Jean Boyd was doing that this year." (page 37)

_____ 7. "She's alone in that world, Wheeze. She needs me." (page 208)

_____ 8. "Why would a woman like you, who could have anything she wanted, come to a place like this?" (page 236)

_____ 9. "Now then, let's try it once more from the beginning—" (page 31)

a. Call

b. Mr. Rice

c. Truitt Bradshaw

d. Susan Bradshaw

e. Sara Louise

f. Caroline

g. Joseph

h. Grandma Bradshaw

i. Captain Wallace

Directions: Choose one of the characters. Write a description of that character. Give your opinion of that character.

32

Written Response

Directions: Think of words and phrases that describe Louise, and put them under her name. Then think of words and phrases that tell how Louise feels about Caroline and Call, and how they feel about her. Label the arrows with these words and phrases.

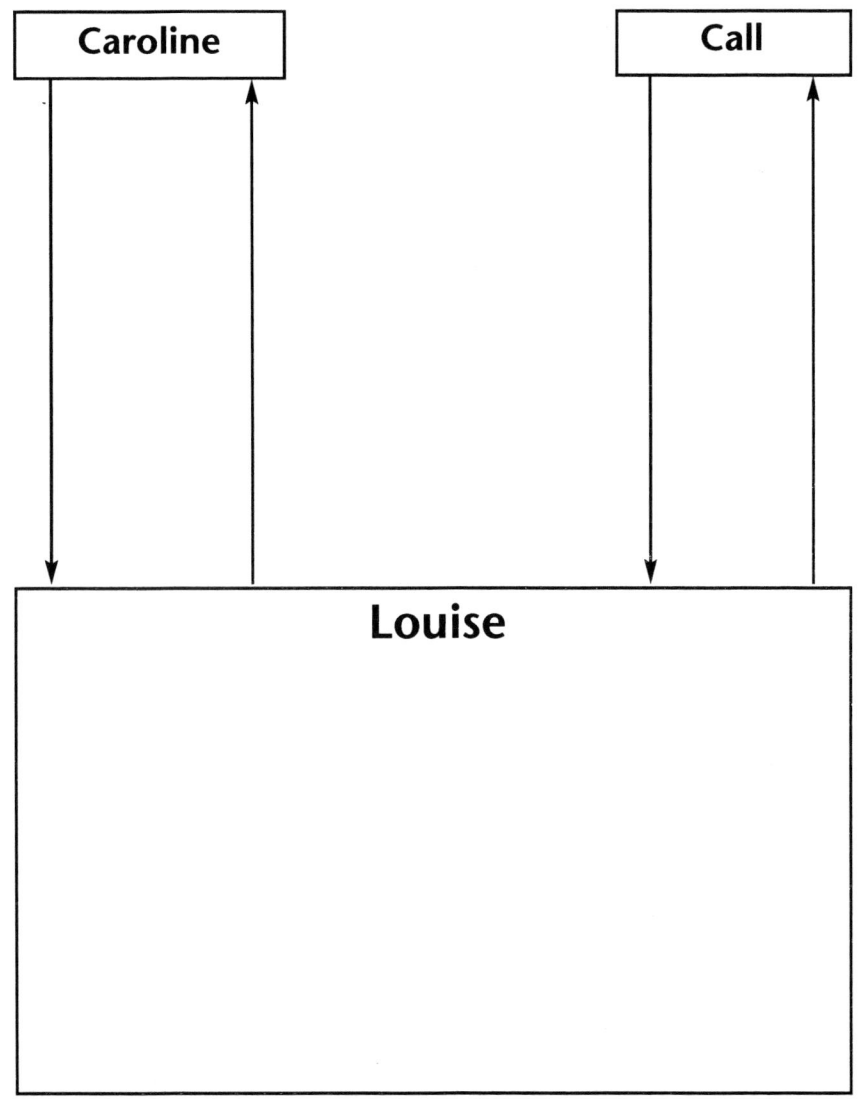

Directions: A *character sketch* is a brief, vivid description of a person. It includes physical characteristics and personality characteristics. Use the notes you have written on the chart above to write a character sketch of Louise.

Written Response

Directions: Select <u>two</u> of the following and write about them. Circle the letters of the two that you select.

A. Captain Wallace gives Louise some advice, telling her, "You don't need anything given to you. You can make your own chances. But first you have to know what you're after, my dear." (page 217) What do you think Captain Wallace means by this?

B. Louise remarks that the people in the mountains "tend to count their wealth in children." (page 232) How would you interpret that remark?

C. Louise thinks that her schoolmates had never cared enough about her "one way or the other" to hate her. (page 191) Explain how this situation might happen.

D. Louise feels that "...there was a certain safety in the unrelenting boredom of each day." (page 146) Do you agree or disagree with Louise? Why?

E. As they prepare the house for the oncoming hurricane, Louise thinks that "...there are things you can do to prepare for a hurricane. It is not like a thunderstorm on the water or a sudden illness before which you are helpless." (page 116) Expand on her thoughts.

F. As the Captain and Louise discuss the future of Trudy's cats, Louise tells the Captain, "A person's got the right to choose their own hazards." (page 105) What do you think Louise means by that statement? What is one "hazard" that you think she has chosen?

G. If the decision were yours to make, what do you think you would do about Trudy Braxton's cats? Why? (pages 104-108)

H. The story is told about a young Hiram Wallace involved in a sudden summer storm, a boat, and fear. The islanders concede that it is proper to have fear when out on the water in a storm. "But fear is one thing. To let fear grab you by the tail and swing you around is another." (page 58) Explain the statement and use Hiram's actions, and the consequences of these actions, as an example.

Multiple Choice

Directions: To the left of each number, write the letter of the BEST response to the question.

_____ 1. Who is telling the story?
A. Caroline Bradshaw
B. Louise Bradshaw
C. Susan Bradshaw
D. Truitt Bradshaw

_____ 2. In what body of water is Rass Island located?
A. Gulf of Mexico
B. Lake Michigan
C. Mississippi River
D. Chesapeake Bay

_____ 3. How old are Louise and Caroline when the story begins?
A. thirteen
B. eighteen
C. twenty-one
D. ten

_____ 4. What compromises the main crops of the Rass Island watermen?
A. corn and beans
B. shark and octopus
C. crabs and oysters
D. trout and bass

_____ 5. What type of land makes up most of Rass Island?
A. salt water marsh
B. desert
C. rain forest
D. mountainous

_____ 6. What nickname does Caroline have for Louise?
A. "S. L."
B. "Junior"
C. "Wheeze"
D. "Crabby"

_____ 7. What represents wealth and security on Rass Island?
   A. boats
   B. money
   C. investments
   D. male children

_____ 8. What is Caroline's "true gift"?
   A. her voice
   B. her computer skills
   C. her investment abilities
   D. her poetic language abilities

_____ 9. What radio announcement alters life on Rass Island in 1941?
   A. bombing of Pearl Harbor
   B. V. E. Day
   C. invasion of Normandy
   D. Battle of the Bulge

_____ 10. Who leaves Rass Island to attend school in Baltimore?
   A. Call
   B. Louise
   C. Caroline
   D. Susan

_____ 11. Who returns to Rass Island after an absence of several years?
   A. Trudy Braxton
   B. Truitt Bradshaw
   C. McCall Purnell
   D. Hiram Wallace

_____ 12. What kind of pets does Auntie Braxton have?
   A. goats
   B. cats
   C. dogs
   D. ducks

_____ 13. What kind of storm hits Rass Island in 1942?
   A. tornado
   B. hurricane
   C. snow
   D. dust

_____ 14. Who does Captain Wallace marry?
   A. Susan Bradshaw
   B. Louise Bradshaw
   C. Caroline Bradshaw
   D. Trudy Braxton

_____ 15. Who joins the Navy during World War II?
   A. Captain Wallace
   B. Truitt Bradshaw
   C. McCall Purnell
   D. Louise Bradshaw

_____ 16. Who attends Juilliard School of Music?
   A. Caroline Bradshaw
   B. Louise Bradshaw
   C. McCall Purnell
   D. Susan Bradshaw

_____ 17. Who attends the University of Maryland and the University of Kentucky?
   A. Caroline Bradshaw
   B. Louise Bradshaw
   C. McCall Purnell
   D. Susan Bradshaw

_____ 18. Who marries McCall Purnell?
   A. Louise Bradshaw
   B. Trudy Braxton
   C. Susan Bradshaw
   D. Caroline Bradshaw

_____ 19. Where does Louise locate after her college graduation?
   A. seashore community
   B. Midwest community
   C. Appalachian community
   D. gold coast community

_____ 20. Who does Louise marry?
   A. Jacob
   B. Hiram
   C. Call
   D. Joseph

Answer Key

Activity # 1: Knowledge Check

1. TRUE
2. FALSE (ATLANTIC)
3. TRUE
4. TRUE
5. FALSE (POTOMAC RIVER)

6. FALSE (CHESAPEAKE BAY BRIDGE)
7. TRUE
8. TRUE
9. FALSE (JOHN SMITH)
10. TRUE

Activity # 2: Freewriting—Student Generated

Study Questions

"Rass Island" & Chapters 1–5, pages 1-72

1. Rass Island is located in the water of the Chesapeake Bay. (page 1) **2.** One has to take a ferry from Crisfield. (page 1) **3.** Crabs are the crop of the watermen in the late spring. (page 2) **4.** The boats tied along the docks are the most important things. (page 2) **5.** Most of the island is a salt water marsh. (page 3) **6.** Chapter 1 begins in the summer of 1941. (page 5) **7.** McCall Purnell is a fourteen year old boy who lives on the island. His father is dead, and he lives with his mother and grandmother. (page 5) **8.** Louise considers Call a good water partner because she can handle the boat and Call can see and catch the crabs and terrapin. Since their teamwork is automatic to Louise, it gives her time to daydream. (page 7-8) **9.** Call never laughs. Louise tries to correct this by telling jokes to Call. However, she has to explain the jokes to Call. (page 8) **10.** Caroline calls Louise "Wheeze." (page 14) **11.** Caroline decides to write a book about her life, because, "once you're famous, information like that is very valuable." She fears if she doesn't get it down, she may forget. (pages 15-16) **12.** Mr. Bradshaw goes to France and gets shrapnel in his hip. When he arrives home, his childhood sweetheart had married someone else. This leaves him free to marry his present wife. (page 17) **13.** Sons represent wealth and security on Rass Island. (page 18) **14.** Caroline had "refused to breathe" at birth, was tiny and fragile. She required hospitalization, and returned to the island when she was two months old. (pages 18-20) **15.** At that time, men's work and women's work are sharply divided, and a waterman's boat was no place for a girl. (page 21) **16.** As a consolation, when Louise is six her father teaches her how to pole a skiff. (page 21) **17.** Susan Bradshaw finds a piano tuner who also gives lessons. He comes to the island once a month and uses the Bradshaw's piano to give lessons to the twins and other island children after tuning the piano. In addition, the children pay twenty cents a week to practice on the piano. (pages 22-23) **18.** "Caroline's true gift was her voice." (page 23) **19.** Mr. Rice takes Caroline to the head of the music department of the college in Salisbury. He takes Caroline as a private pupil and waives the fee. (page 24) **20.** Louise hears about the Japanese attack on Pearl Harbor. (page 27) **21.** Mrs. Bradshaw serves coffee to the twins for the first time in their lives. (page 29) **22.** Louise feels that Christmas should be canceled. The students laugh at her, and Mr. Rice continues on with the practice. (pages 30-31) **23.** The stranger brings a valise, two additional bags and a small trunk. This indicates that he plans to stay for a long time. (page 49) **24.** The older people on the island surmise that the stranger is Hiram Wallace. (page 54) **25.** The stranger is friendly, and invites Louise and Call inside for tea. (pages 66-67) **26.** After hearing their names, the stranger refers to them as "Wheeze and Cough." This makes Call laugh. (page 69) **27.** Louise and Call decide to call the stranger "Captain." (page 71)

Chapters 6–10, pages 73-125

28. Louise hates Caroline because Caroline will not fight with her. (page 74) **29.** Louise plans to double her crab catch, save half of the money she earns, and send herself to boarding school in Crisfield. (pages 76-77) **30.** Louise enters a song lyric contest. (page 78) **31.** It is decided the Call and Louise would help the Captain two hours every day except Sunday. They would receive no pay. (pages 88-89) **32.** February is Louise's least favorite winter month. It strikes "punch after punch." (page 91) **33.** Louise's least favorite summer month is August because of its heat and haze. (page 92) **34.** The Captain's one concession to the August temperature is that the work may be done indoors. (page 93) **35.** Louise receives a letter that tells her she is a winner, but not a money prize winner. She is then asked to send in $25.00 to have her lyrics published, etc. (pages 93-94) **36.** The Captain tells Louise and Call that the Bible does not say how one should speak to cats. (page 96) **37.** The Captain calls Auntie Braxton by her first name. This gives Louise a feeling of pleasure. (page 97) **38.** Louise sees Auntie Braxton on the floor, with cats crawling over her. Louise assumes that Auntie Braxton is dead. (page 98) **39.** The Captain goes to Auntie Braxton. She is alive. (page 99) **40.** The Captain comforts Auntie, and calls her by her first name in front of other island men who are also helping her. (pages 100-101) **41.** The cats cause the biggest problem for the Captain, Louise and Call. (page 102) **42.** The Captain initially decides to drown the cats. (page 105) **43.** Caroline suggests that the cats be drugged and then given away. This plan works. (pages 112-114) **44.** The windows of the house are boarded up, food is moved upstairs, the stove is turned off, and the boat is made fast. They also help the Captain prepare his house. (pages 115-117) **45.** Louise goes to get the Captain. He sits out the storm at the Bradshaws' home. (page 120) **46.** Caroline sleeps through the storm. (page 122) **47.** The storm reduces the cat population "by at least two-thirds." (page 125)

Chapters 11–15, pages 126-193
48. Students' opinions will vary. **49.** "Nothing was left at the spot where the Captain's house had stood the night before." (page 130) **50.** They need to know if the boat is all right. (page 135) Student opinion.
51. The Captain lives with the Bradshaws for three days. (page 139) **52.** The Captain arranges to live in Trudy's house while he cleans it. (pages 144-145) **53.** Louise's theory is that the hands are the most revealing part of the human body. (page 147) Student opinion. **54.** Students' opinions will vary.
55. Students' opinions will vary. **56.** Louise thinks that "crazy people who are judged to be harmless are allowed an enormous amount of freedom ordinary people are denied." (page 151) Student opinion.
57. Caroline suggests to the Captain that he marry Miss Trudy. (page 157) Caroline points out to the Captain that Miss Trudy needs him. (page 158) **58.** Louise is upset. She feels that, if alcohol were available to her, she would become a drunk. (page 162) **59.** Caroline sings for the Captain and Trudy. (page 167) **60.** Call drops out of school because his mother and grandmother are destitute. Call goes to work for Mr. Bradshaw. (page 171) **61.** Call grows taller and thinner; his manner changes and he seems more dignified. (page 172) **62.** The Captain proposes to send Caroline to a boarding school with a good music department so she can continue her voice lessons. (pages 176-177) **63.** Louise is saddened and thinks that the Captain is like everyone else—choosing Caroline over her. (page 180) **64.** Susan Bradshaw offers to send Louise to school in Crisfield. Louise turns down the offer. (page 182) **65.** After Call joins the navy, Louise takes over the responsibility of her father's crab floats. (page 183) When school starts in the fall, Louise does not return. (page 185) **66.** Louise spends the winter on the *Portia Sue* with her father. She is content and happy. (pages 187-188) **67.** When dredging is done, the muck and trash and the ocean bottom is cranked up with the oysters, thereby disturbing the oyster bed. Tonging causes little disturbance of the oyster bed. (page 189) **68.** Mrs. Bradshaw teaches Louise at home, and the Captain teaches Louise math. (pages 191-192)

Chapters 16–20, pages 194-244
69. Call has "growed up." He is "tall and almost shockingly broad-shouldered and thin-hipped..." (page 201) **70.** Call tells Louise that "the water's about to get her [the island]." He thinks that the next good storm will be the end of the island. (page 202) **71.** Call says, "You never did think I was much to brag about, now did you?" (page 208) Student opinion. **72.** Louise stays home from the wedding to care for her grandmother. This also gives Mr. and Mrs. Bradshaw time to be together. (pages 209-210) **73.** Louise learns that her grandmother had a crush on the Captain when she was young. She tells Louise, "He run off and left before I had a chance," and the Captain, "One time I was too young and too poor for you to pay me any mind." (pages 211-212 & 215) **74.** The Captain tells Louise that she is not meant to be on the island—that she can do anything she wants to do, but she has to know what it is she wants. (pages 216-218) Student opinion. **75.** It is inferred that Mr. and Mrs. Bradshaw have a close, loving relationship. (pages 219-221) **76.** Students' opinions and reasons will vary. (pages 224-226) **77.** Louise wants her mother to allow her to leave the island. (pages 226-227) **78.** Louise decides to go to college. She would like to be a doctor. (pages 229-230) Louise is forced to change her plans and to go to nursing school because the chances for any woman to get into medical school at that time are "practically nonexistent." (page 231) **79.** Louise decides to locate in Truitt, an Appalachian community in need of a nurse-

midwife. The village is in a valley completely surrounded by mountains. She plans to work there for 2 or 3 years, and then to apply for medical school. (pages 231-232) **80.** The school is large in Truitt because there are more families there. People in Truitt "tend to count their wealth in children." (page 232) Opinions will vary. **81.** The most pressing health problem in Truitt is caused by the men who get drunk and beat their wives and children. (page 233) Louise feels that the men of Truitt fight the land for an existence and struggle against their mountains. "On Rass men followed the water." (page 233) **82.** Louise meets Joseph when he comes to ask that she come to treat his son, Stephen. (page 234) **83.** Joseph surmises that Louise has been preparing all of her life to come to live in the mountains. (page 236) **84.** Louise concludes that Joseph is the man that she will marry after she sees him smile. "For when he smiled, he looked like the kind of man who would sing to the oysters." (page 237) **85.** Louise's son is named Truitt, after her father, but the townspeople assume that the child is named after the town. This makes the people take Louise into their hearts. (page 240) Opinion—answers will vary. **86.** Students' opinions will vary. (page 242)   39**87.** Students' opinions will vary. (page 244) **88.** Students' opinions. Answers will vary.

Activities
Activity # 3: Similes—Student Generated

Activity # 4: Vocabulary—Synonym or Antonym?
1. BEWILDERED   5. DISTINCTIVE   9. BENEVOLENTLY
2. MEAGER   6. RANKLE   10. PRECARIOUS
3. AFFLUENT   7. AVID   11. STRENUOUSLY
4. DELUSIONS   8. VULGAR   12. EXQUISITE

Activity # 5: Vocabulary—Scrambled Words
1. undaunted e - resolute
2. emphatic c - accentuated
3. semblance a- appearance
4. coincidences h - chances
5. deceptively b - seemingly
6. lugubriously g - dismally
7. benevolently d- kindly
8. consolation f - assuagement

Activity # 6: Vocabulary Kriss Kross
1. frivolous   10. exasperated

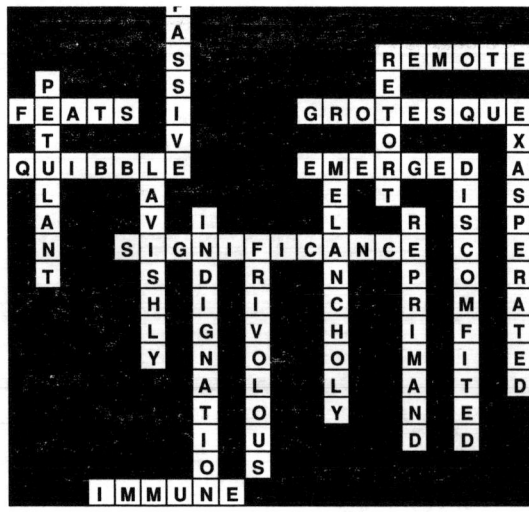

2. grotesque   11. reprimand
3. significance   12. feats
4. emerged   13. passive
5. discomfited   14. indignation
6. lavishly   15. petulant
7. remote   16. melancholy
8. immune   17. retort
9. quibble

Activity # 7: Vocabulary Blending Syllables

<table>
<tr><td>1. terrapin</td><td>6. emphatic</td><td>11. polonaise</td></tr>
<tr><td>2. distinctive</td><td>7. loblolly</td><td>12. remonstrance</td></tr>
<tr><td>3. delusions</td><td>8. undaunted</td><td>13. petulant</td></tr>
<tr><td>4. consumption</td><td>9. exquisite</td><td>14. mediate</td></tr>
<tr><td>5. looniness</td><td>10. bewildered</td><td>15. reprimand</td></tr>
</table>

Activity # 8: Vocabulary Expanding Words

<table>
<tr><td>1. PRIMLY</td><td>6. PRECARIOUS</td><td>11. NAUSEATED</td></tr>
<tr><td>2. DISTINCTIVE</td><td>7. LOONINESS</td><td>12. SHRAPNEL</td></tr>
<tr><td>3. BRACKISH</td><td>8. THWART</td><td>13. MEAGER</td></tr>
<tr><td>4. FINANCE</td><td>9. UNDAUNTED</td><td>14. BEWILDER</td></tr>
<tr><td>5. CONSUMPTION</td><td>10. BASKING</td><td>15. AFFLUENT</td></tr>
</table>

Activity # 9: Vocabulary

1. T H W A R T
     4   5 15 13   12

2. D E L U S I O N S
     19   3   2 18

3. B A S K I N G
       8 7

4. P R I M L Y
    11 6 9 14 1

5. C O N S U M P T I O N
     10   17   16

Y O U T H I S A M O R T A L W O U N D
1 2 3 4 5 6 7 8 9 10 11 12 13 14 15 16 17 18 19

Activity # 10: Vocabulary—Puzzlement

<table>
<tr><td>1. interloper</td><td>6. significance</td></tr>
<tr><td>2. pretentious</td><td>7. unproscribed</td></tr>
<tr><td>3. formulated</td><td>8. remonstrance</td></tr>
<tr><td>4. dilapidated</td><td>9. undefinable</td></tr>
<tr><td>5. machinations</td><td>10. ramshackle</td></tr>
</table>

Activity # 11: Vocabulary Crossword

Activity # 12: Vocabulary—Synonym Chains Student Generated

Activity # 13: Vocabulary—Missing Vowels

1. SAVAGERY - 126
2. REASSURING - 129
3. PRISSY - 146
4. DENIED - 151
5. DELICACY - 158
6. RAMPAGES - 169
7. MOULT - 184
8. RESIDUE - 192
9. TENDRIL - 198
10. FLOES - 127
11. TRAGEDY - 135
12. DISEMBODIED - 147
13. FILTHIEST - 154
14. HAWKING - 165
(continued on next page)
15. DESTITUTE - 171

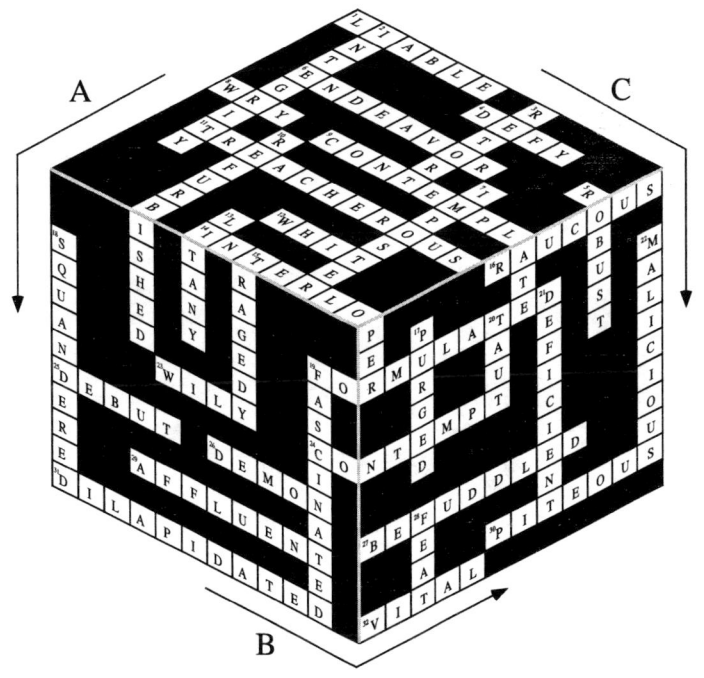

41

16. JEOPARDY - 185
17. SLOSHING - 196
18. MARVELOUSLY - 201

Activity # 14: Mathematics

1. four (80 cents / 20 cents = 4 children)
2. $41.60 (52 X $.80)
3. $2.00 (4 X $.50)
4. $24.00 (12 X $2.00)
5. 4 wks. $1.30 ($.50 + $.80)   5 wks. $1.50 ($.50 + $1.00)
6. five cents for each crab ($.50/10)
   Louise & Call have caught 88 crabs ($2.45 x 2 = $4.90 - $.50 [terrapin] = $4.40 for crabs/$.05 = 88)
7. 20 crabs (she gets paid 1/2 of the money)
8. 30 crabs (she gets paid 1/3 of the money)
9. Student Generated

Activity # 15: Mathematics

1. Value of each crab = $0.15   300% ($0.15/$0.05 X 100 = 300%)
2. 200% ($0.30/$0.15 X 100 = 200%)   600% ($0.30/$0.05 X 100 = 600%)
3. $1.20 ($1.25 - $0.05   416 2/3 % ($1.25/$0.30 X 100 + 416 2/3%)
   2500% ($1.25/$0.05 X 100 = 2500%)   220% ($2.75/$1.25 X 100 = 220%)

Student Generated Ad

Activity # 16: Words and Phrases—Student Generated

Activity # 17: Cryptogram

LIFE,   LIKE   A   CRAB   POT,   CATCHES   A   LOT
OLIH,   OLNH   D   FUDE   SRW,   FDWFKHV   D   ORW

OF   TRASH   YOU   HAVEN'T   BARGAINED   FOR.
RI   WUDVK   BRX   KDYHQ'W   EDUJDLQHG   IRU.

Activity # 18: Word Search Puzzle—Vocabulary Review

Hidden Message: HE LOOKED LIKE THE KIND OF MAN WHO WOULD SING TO THE OYSTERS X
(Where X = period)

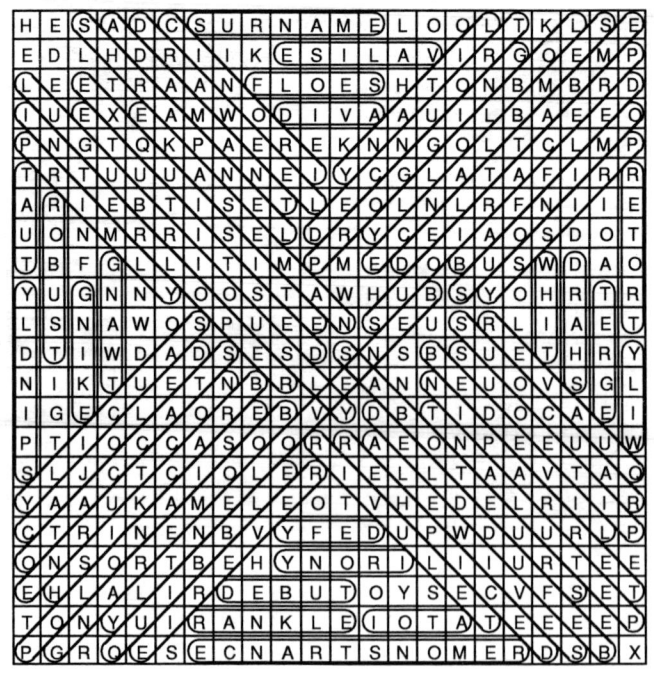

Activity # 19: Story Review

1 = O	5 = H	9 = E	13 = S
2 = N	6 = U	10 = R	14 = G
3 = I	7 = D	11 = W	15 = M
4 = T	8 = F	12 = A	16 = C

I F O U N D T H E R E W A S N O T H I N G M U C H T O F I N D
3 8 1 6 2 7 4 5 9 10 9 11 12 13 2 1 4 5 3 2 14 15 6 16 5 4 1 83 2 7

Activity # 20: Story Review Crossword Puzzle

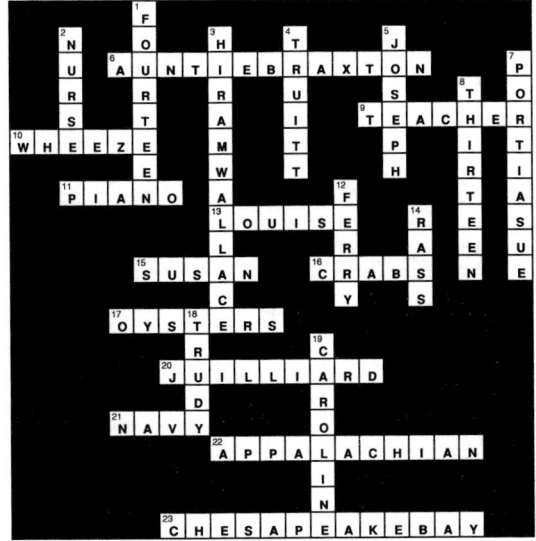

Tests

Comprehension Quiz: True—False

1. T
2. F (LOUISE)
3. F (LOUISE & CAROLINE)
4. T
5. T
6. F (PIANO)
7. F (HIRAM WALLACE)
8. T
9. F (LOUISE)
10. T
11. F (LOUISE)
12. T
13. T
14. F (CAROLINE)
15. T

Comprehension Quiz: Short Answer

1. The Captain's property is destroyed during the hurricane.
2. The Captain arranges to live in Trudy's house while he cleans it.
3. Caroline encourages the Captain to marry Trudy.
4. Louise is upset and would have turned to alcohol had it been available to her.
5. Call's mother and grandmother are destitute, and Call needs to earn some money.
6. The Captain proposes to send Caroline to a school in Baltimore that has a good music department.
7. Louise takes over Call's responsibilities, starting with the crab floats.
8. Louise is taught by her mother and the Captain.
9. Call predicts that the water will "get" [destroy] the island.
10. Louise stays home to care for Grandma Bradshaw.
11. Louise gets a scholarship to the University of Maryland.
12. The chances for a girl getting into medical school at that time were "practically nonexistent."
13. Louise moves to the town of Truitt, an Appalachian community in need of a nurse-midwife.
14. The most pressing health problem in Truitt is alcohol, which causes the men who get drunk to beat their wives.
15. Louise concludes that Joseph is the man she will marry.

Novel Test: Vocabulary

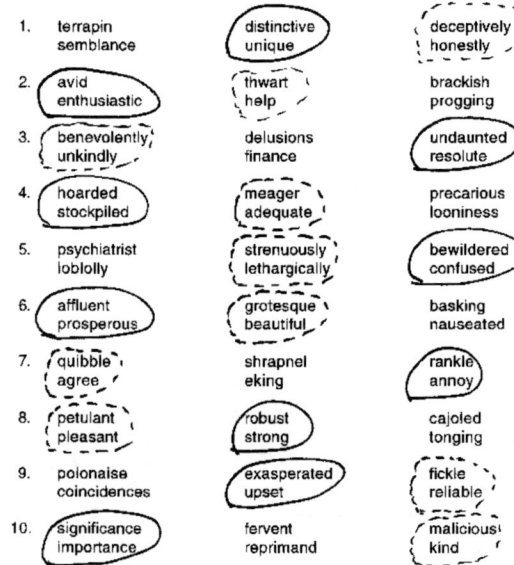

1. terrapin
   semblance

   distinctive
   unique

   deceptively
   honestly

2. avid
   enthusiastic

   thwart
   help

   brackish
   progging

3. benevolently
   unkindly

   delusions
   finance

   undaunted
   resolute

4. hoarded
   stockpiled

   meager
   adequate

   precarious
   looniness

5. psychiatrist
   loblolly

   strenuously
   lethargically

   bewildered
   confused

6. affluent
   prosperous

   grotesque
   beautiful

   basking
   nauseated

7. quibble
   agree

   shrapnel
   eking

   rankle
   annoy

8. petulant
   pleasant

   robust
   strong

   cajoled
   tonging

9. polonaise
   coincidences

   exasperated
   upset

   fickle
   reliable

10. significance
    importance

    fervent
    reprimand

    malicious
    kind

Novel Test: Identification By Clues

1 - c - Susan Bradshaw
2 - g - Call
3 - f - Captain Wallace
4 - i - Grandma Bradshaw
5 - h - Caroline
6 - b - Auntie Braxton
7 - e - Truitt Bradshaw
8 - a - Louise
9 - d - Joseph

Novel Test: Identification By Quotation

1 - e - Sara Louise
2 - h - Grandma Bradshaw
3 - d - Susan Bradshaw
4 - i - Captain Wallace
5 - c - Truitt Bradshaw
6 - f - Caroline
7 - a - Call
8 - g - Joseph
9 - b - Mr. Rice

Novel Test: Written Response—Literary Analysis—Student Generated

Novel Test: Written Response—Critical and Creative Thinking—Student Generated

Novel Test: Multiple Choice

1 - B (LOUISE BRADSHAW)
2 - D (CHESAPEAKE BAY)
3 - A (THIRTEEN)
4 - C (CRABS AND OYSTERS)
5 - A (SALT WATER MARSH)
6 - C (WHEEZE)
7 - D (MALE CHILDREN)
8 - A (HER VOICE)
9 - A (BOMBING OF PEARL HARBOR)
10 - C (CAROLINE)
11 - D (HIRAM WALLACE)
12 - B (CATS)
13 - B (HURRICANE)
14 - D (TRUDY BRAXTON)
15 - C (McCALL PURNELL)
16 - A (CAROLINE BRADSHAW)
17 - B (LOUISE BRADSHAW)
18 - D (CAROLINE BRADSHAW)
19 - C (APPALACHIAN COMMUNITY)
20 - D (JOSEPH)